A LIFEGUIDE  BIBLE STUDY

# MARK

## Follow Me

*22 Studies in 2 Parts
for individuals or groups*

### James Hoover

With Notes for Leaders

INTERVARSITY PRESS
DOWNERS GROVE, ILLINOIS 60515

© *1985 by Inter-Varsity Christian Fellowship of the United States of America*

*All rights reserved. No part of this book may be reproduced in any form without written permission from InterVarsity Press, Downers Grove, Illinois.*

*InterVarsity Press is the book-publishing division of Inter-Varsity Christian Fellowship, a student movement active on campus at hundreds of universities, colleges and schools of nursing. For information about local and regional activities, write IVCF, 233 Langdon St., Madison, WI 53703.*

*Cover photograph: Robert McKendrick*

*ISBN 0-8308-1004-8*

*Printed in the United States of America*

| 20 | 19 | 18 | 17 | 16 | 15 | 14 | 13 | 12 | 11 | 10 | 9 |
|----|----|----|----|----|----|----|----|----|----|----|---|
| 99 | 98 | 97 | 96 | 95 | 94 | 93 | | | | | |

# Contents

# Getting the Most
# from LifeGuide Bible Studies

Many of us long to fill our minds and our lives with Scripture. We desire to be transformed by its message. LifeGuide Bible Studies are designed to be an exciting and challenging way to do just that. They help us to be guided by God's Word in every area of life.

## How They Work

LifeGuides have a number of distinctive features. Perhaps the most important is that they are *inductive* rather than *deductive*. In other words, they lead us to *discover* what the Bible says rather than simply *telling* us what it says.

They are also thought provoking. They help us to think about the meaning of the passage so that we can truly understand what the author is saying. The questions require more than one-word answers.

The studies are personal. Questions expose us to the promises, assurances, exhortations and challenges of God's Word. They are designed to allow the Scriptures to renew our minds so that we can be transformed by the Spirit of God. This is the ultimate goal of all Bible study.

The studies are versatile. They are designed for student, neighborhood and church groups. They are also effective for individual study.

## How They're Put Together

LifeGuides also have a distinctive format. Each study need take no more than forty-five minutes in a group setting or thirty minutes in personal study—unless you choose to take more time.

The studies can be used within a quarter system in a church and fit well in a semester or trimester system on a college campus. If a guide has more than thirteen studies, it is divided into two or occasionally three parts of approximately twelve studies each.

LifeGuides use a workbook format. Space is provided for writing answers to each question. This is ideal for personal study and allows group members to prepare in advance for the discussion. The studies also contain leader's notes. They show how to lead a group discussion, provide additional background information on certain questions, give helpful tips on group dynamics and suggest ways to deal with problems which may arise during the discussion. With such helps, someone with little or no experience can lead an effective study.

## Suggestions for Individual Study

1. As you begin each study, pray that God will help you to understand and apply the passage to your life.

2. Read and reread the assigned Bible passage to familiarize yourself with what the author is saying. In the case of book studies, you may want to read through the entire book prior to the first study. This will give you a helpful overview of its contents.

3. A good modern translation of the Bible, rather than the King James Version or a paraphrase, will give you the most help. The New International Version, the New American Standard Bible and the Revised Standard Version are all recommended. However, the questions in this guide are based on the New International Version.

4. Write your answers in the space provided in the study guide. This will help you to express your understanding of the passage clearly.

5. It might be good to have a Bible dictionary handy. Use it to look up any unfamiliar words, names or places.

## Suggestions for Group Study

1. Come to the study prepared. Follow the suggestions for individual study mentioned above. You will find that careful preparation will greatly enrich your time spent in group discussion.

2. Be willing to participate in the discussion. The leader of your group will not be lecturing. Instead, he or she will be encouraging the members of the group to discuss what they have learned from the passage. The leader will be asking the questions that are found in this guide. Plan to share what God has taught you in your individual study.

3. Stick to the passage being studied. Your answers should be based on the verses which are the focus of the discussion and not on outside authorities such as commentaries or speakers. This guide deliberately avoids jumping

from book to book or passage to passage. Each study focuses on only one passage. Book studies are generally designed to lead you through the book in the order in which it was written. This will help you follow the author's argument.

4. Be sensitive to the other members of the group. Listen attentively when they share what they have learned. You may be surprised by their insights! Link what you say to the comments of others so the group stays on the topic. Also, be affirming whenever you can. This will encourage some of the more hesitant members of the group to participate.

5. Be careful not to dominate the discussion. We are sometimes so eager to share what we have learned that we leave too little opportunity for others to respond. By all means participate! But allow others to also.

6. Expect God to teach you through the passage being discussed and through the other members of the group. Pray that you will have an enjoyable and profitable time together.

7. If you are the discussion leader, you will find additional suggestions and helpful ideas for each study in the leader's notes. These are found at the back of the guide.

# Introducing Mark

Few Americans put much stock in royalty. We have been raised to treasure the spirit of democracy. But democracy, at least on any large scale, is a recent development in human history. People in other eras were most accustomed to kings. For good or evil, kings and emperors left their mark on daily life. Thus when a new king came to power, whether through natural succession or through defeat in battle, questions clamored in people's minds. What would the new king be like? Would he be kind and compassionate or selfish and ruthless? Would he use his power to serve his own ends, or would he seek the welfare of all his subjects?

The Jews of Jesus' day, long oppressed by foreign rulers, yearned for a new king—one whom God himself would anoint and use to establish his own rule of justice and peace, not only over Israel, but over all the earth. Imagine the excitement then as John the Baptist came announcing the coming of the Lord as king and as Jesus himself announced, "The time has come. The kingdom of God is near." Yet as Jesus continued his ministry he met a growing wave of opposition. Not everyone was pleased with the kind of kingdom he seemed to be announcing or with who he proclaimed himself to be. The religious rulers especially opposed him, but the common people heard him gladly.

New Testament scholars, with few exceptions, agree that Mark's Gospel is the earliest written account of Jesus' life and ministry. Composed between A.D. 60 and 70, it likely served as the basis for the Gospels of Matthew and Luke. Mark himself, though not one of the Twelve, was probably an early convert (Acts 12:12) and a companion to both Peter (1 Pet 5:13) and Paul. Though Mark had an early falling out with Paul (Acts 15:36-41), the two were clearly reconciled later on (Col 4:10; 2 Tim 4:11; Philem 24). Thus Mark is linked to two of the most prominent apostles.

More and more, scholars are coming to believe that Mark was not just a collector of stories about Jesus but that he gave form and shape to these stories to counteract some dangerous distortions of the gospel message.[1] Apparently some Christians so focused on Jesus' deity and glorious resurrection that they began to ignore his humanity and suffering. As a result they expected to be spared suffering in this life and to quickly join Jesus in the glories of heaven. You can well imagine how their faith may have been shaken when Nero took to using some of them as torches!

Mark, theologically and pastorally, sets out to retell the story of Jesus, showing that the kingdom in its glory comes at the end of the path of suffering and service. While Matthew focuses on Jesus as the teacher from whom we should learn (Mt 11:29; 28:20) and John focuses on him as the Son of God in whom we should believe (Jn 20:31), Mark portrays Jesus principally as the servant-king whom we should follow (Mk 1:17). Thus, if we are to enjoy the glories of the kingdom, we too must follow the road of suffering and service.

This guide offers you the opportunity to learn through the eyes of Mark more about Jesus and the life he calls each of us to. It consists of twenty-two forty-five-minute studies. The studies have been divided into two parts, ten in the first and twelve in the second, so that the whole Gospel can easily be studied in two quarters. The last study in each part is a review to help summarize and tie together major themes from that portion of the Gospel. Although these studies have been designed with believers in mind, they have been successfully used, with minor changes, in a mixed group of believers and inquirers into the faith.

May the Lord himself increase your understanding of who he is and the life to which he has called you.

---

[1]For a survey of literature through 1971, see Ralph Martin, *Mark: Evangelist and Theologian* (Grand Rapids, Mich.: Zondervan, 1973).

# Part 1
# Who Is Jesus?

## Mark 1—8

# 1
# Gospel Beginnings
## *Mark 1:1-13*

Do you have any friends who begin mystery novels at the back? Like endings, beginnings tell us a lot. In them writers set the context for what is to come and often drop hints which later prove to be important. The beginning of Mark's Gospel is no exception. This study introduces several important themes which will be developed in the following chapters.

**1.** What stories, pictures or objects in your family link you to past generations? What importance does this sense of history have for you?

**2.** Read Mark 1:1-13. What does verse 1 reveal about Mark's own view of the events he is about to describe?

**3.** Verses 2 and 3 combine quotations from Malachi and Isaiah. What do these two quotations have in common?

In what context do they put the events Mark is about to describe?

**4.** Verses 2 and 3 suggest preparations being made for the coming of a king. Drawing together evidence from the whole passage, determine who is sending out his messenger (the "I" of v. 2).

Who does Mark suggest the coming king is? Who is the messenger?

**5.** How does John's ministry prepare the way for Jesus?

**6.** Malachi 4:5 describes this messenger as one having a ministry like that of the prophet Elijah. (For the account of Elijah's ministry see 1 Kings 17— 2 Kings 2.) In what ways does Mark emphasize the similarities between John and Elijah?

**7.** Malachi wrote more than 400 years before the coming of Jesus, and Isaiah wrote almost 400 years before Malachi. What difference does it make to you that the good news is so deeply rooted in history?

**8.** How did the crowd respond to John? What does the crowd's response suggest about their sense of need?

**9.** How does John emphasize the greatness of the one who will come after him (vv. 7-8)?

**10.** Despite his greatness Jesus came to John for baptism. What does this tell us about Jesus' relationship to us?

**11.** How do the events surrounding Jesus' baptism prepare him for his temptation in the desert?

**12.** Many of Mark's readers in Rome were facing wild animals in the arena under the Neronian persecutions. How do you think they responded to Mark's description of Jesus' temptation (vv. 12-13)?

What encouragement do you find here for facing your own temptations?

**13.** How has Mark set the scene thus far for what's to come?

**14.** Ask God to prepare you more fully for the coming of the king through the study of Mark's Gospel.

# 2
# Four
# Portraits

## *Mark 1:14-39*

Wall live with authority—whether supervisors, professors, parents, police. And depending on how that authority is exercised, we feel either put upon, trapped, used, or we feel secure, free and useful.

In 1:1-13 Mark has told us that Jesus has come as king to fulfill the Old Testament longings for the Lord's rule over all the earth. But what kind of king is he? Mark, it seems, knows that a picture is worth a thousand words. So, rather than offering an abstract character analysis, he paints four verbal portraits of Jesus in action.

---

**1.** Think of those who have authority over your life—parents, employer, teachers, the government. Is your response to their authority usually positive or negative? Explain why.

---

**2.** Read Mark 1:14-39 and see if you can discover what these four portraits have in common.

---

**3.** We often think of the gospel solely as a message about the forgiveness of sins. Yet Jesus began his ministry proclaiming a different kind of good news. What was his good news and what response did it call for (vv. 14-15)?

---

**4.** What different factors contributed to the ready response of Simon and Andrew, James and John to Jesus' invitation (vv. 16-20)? (Don't forget 1:1-13!)

How does Jesus' command "follow me" summarize the essence of discipleship?

---

**5.** On the Sabbath Jesus goes to the synagogue (vv. 21-28). What happens while he is there and how do the people respond?

What might be some of the reasons that Jesus silences the demon about who he is?

---

**6.** What impression of Jesus do you get from the portrait of his visit to the home of Simon and Andrew (vv. 29-34)?

---

**7.** Thus far we have looked at three portraits of Jesus. What aspects of Jesus' character do we see in them?

**8.** Which aspect of Jesus' character is most prominent in these three incidents?

How has Mark emphasized this trait?

**9.** How do these accounts of Jesus' activity relate to his announcement in verse 15?

**10.** How does Jesus exercise his authority differently from kings and dictators and other human authorities?

What practical differences can knowing this make in your own response to Jesus' authority?

**11.** The quiet and solitude of verses 35-39 are quite a contrast from the previous events. What do these verses reveal about Jesus' priorities?

What steps do you need to take to bring your priorities more closely in line with his?

# 3
# A Leper, a Paralytic and a Tax Collector

## *Mark 1:40—2:17*

U nclean! Unclean!" the man shouted, and everyone scattered to avoid contact with the leper—everyone except Jesus.

The religious wisdom of the day demanded that a holy man keep away from the common people, the "sinners." So Jesus was bound to encounter resistance as he openly welcomed them. This passage focuses on Christ's compassion toward those we normally avoid.

**1.** What type of person in our society would you feel most uncomfortable associating with? Explain why.

**2.** Read Mark 1:40—2:17. Notice how the pace slows down, and see if you can spot the main cause of the resistance Jesus faces.

**3.** Leviticus 13:45-46 states that a leper "must wear torn clothes, let his hair be unkempt, cover the lower part of his face and cry out, 'Unclean! Unclean!' As long as he has the infection he remains unclean. He must live alone; he must live outside the camp." How then would this disease have affected the man psychologically, religiously and socially?

**4.** What risks did the leper take in coming to Jesus (1:40-45)?

What risks did Jesus take in responding to him as he did?

**5.** How does Jesus respond to the man's total need?

**6.** Imagine that you are the paralytic being lowered before Jesus (2:1-12). How do you feel, especially when Jesus announces, "Son, your sins are forgiven"?

How do you feel after you have been healed?

**7.** In what ways does Jesus' healing of the paralytic answer the questions raised in the minds of the teachers of the law?

**8.** The paralytic's friends provide a model of caring. What are some practical ways we can follow their example?

**9.** Contrast the Pharisees' attitude toward tax collectors and "sinners" with that of Jesus.

**10.** In his reply to the Pharisees' complaint, Jesus specifically likens himself to a doctor. How has he acted as a doctor throughout this passage?

**11.** How is sin like illness, especially leprosy and paralysis?

**12.** Jesus came announcing the kingdom and calling people to follow him. What change would need to take place in these Pharisees before they could answer Jesus' call?

**13.** Who do you consider to be some of the "unlovely" or "unreachable" for God's kingdom?

What steps can you take to bring your thinking and actions toward them into line with those of Jesus?

# 4
# Conflict in Galilee
## *Mark 2:18—3:35*

A truly religious person wouldn't do such a thing!"

"Religion is fine, but you're becoming a fanatic!"

Such accusations are commonly leveled at Christians. They are difficult to bear under any circumstances. But when they come from family and friends, the pain is even greater.

In the last study we saw the beginning of opposition to Jesus and his ministry. Now that opposition gains momentum, from the Pharisees and even Jesus' own family. This passage looks at some of the pressures and privileges of following Jesus.

**1.** The Bible promises that every follower of Jesus will eventually face persecution. What types of opposition have you encountered as a Christian?

**2.** Read Mark 2:18—3:35. On what grounds are Jesus and his disciples criticized in 2:18—3:6?

**3.** In verses 19-22, how does Jesus explain his disciples' failure to fast?

**4.** How are Jesus' and the Pharisees' attitudes toward the Sabbath different?

**5.** How do Jesus' comments in verses 27-28 rebuke both too rigid and too lax a view of the Sabbath?

**6.** What is ironic about the Pharisees' reaction to Jesus' healing on the Sabbath (3:1-6)?

**7.** The Pharisees objected to what Jesus and his disciples did and failed to do. What objections might people today have toward what we do or fail to do as Christians?

How can Jesus' responses to opposition be a model for our own responses?

**8.** While the Pharisees and the Herodians are plotting to kill Jesus, how are the common people responding to him (3:7-12)?

**9.** Explain how Jesus' plans for the twelve apostles (3:14-15) fit in with his original call to the four fishermen in Galilee (1:17).

**10.** What charge do the teachers of the law bring against Jesus in 3:20-30? How does Jesus refute it?

**11.** Mark indicates that Jesus gave the teachers of the law this warning about blaspheming against the Holy Spirit because they were saying he had an evil or unclean spirit. By charging Jesus with having an evil spirit, how were they approaching the brink of total and unforgivable blindness to the truth?

**12.** Jesus' mother and brothers come for him because they think he is out of his mind (3:21, 31-32). How do you think this made Jesus feel?

**13.** When we are opposed or rejected by those who are closest to us, what comfort can we receive from Jesus' words in verses 33-35?

**14.** If we learn to see ourselves as part of God's family, rather than merely his slaves or subjects, how might that transform our attitude toward his commandments?

# 5
# Kingdom Parables

## *Mark 4:1-34*

Some stories wear their points on their sleeves, as it were. Others, to borrow from P. G. Wodehouse's definition of a parable, keep something up their sleeves "which suddenly pops up and knocks you flat." Among Jesus' stories we find a variety—from those that are easy to understand to those that are so difficult they invite our thought and reflection again and again. The stories in this passage contain vital information about God's kingdom and its subjects—for those who have ears to hear!

**1.** Mark Twain once said, "It's not the parts of the Bible I don't understand that bother me, but the parts I do understand!" How does your attitude compare with his?

**2.** Read Mark 4:1-34, watching especially for words and phrases that are repeated in verses 1-25. What idea or ideas seem to dominate these verses?

**3.** Jesus explains the parable of the sower, or the parable of the soils (vv. 3-8), in verses 14-20. Put this explanation in your own words, describing from your own experience examples of each kind of soil-seed combination.

---

**4.** Verses 11-12 have long bothered many readers. The problem is that it looks like Jesus is saying that he tells parables to keep people from seeking forgiveness. From the context, which seems more likely—that verse 12 expresses the *reason* that Jesus speaks in parables or simply *what happens* when he does? Explain your answer.

---

**5.** To whom does Jesus explain the parable of the soils (vv. 10-12)?

What did they do to get an explanation that the others did not?

---

**6.** What does a willingness to ask indicate about a willingness to hear?

On what grounds then are people included or excluded from the secret of the kingdom?

---

**7.** What is the secret of the kingdom?

**8.** How does the response Jesus gets from telling the parable of the sower illustrate the point he is making?

**9.** What kind of soil are you?

What can you do to become the kind of soil Jesus is looking for?

**10.** The farmer was not being foolish in sowing the seed where he did. He was following the standard practice of the day—sowing then plowing. Only as time passed did each kind of soil reveal itself for what it was. What encouragement does this give you to "sow widely" as you share the good news of the kingdom with others?

**11.** How do verses 21-25 help explain verses 11-12?

**12.** What insights into kingdom growth do the parables of the growing seed and the mustard seed give us (vv. 26-34)?

**13.** In this passage we see Jesus both spreading the message of the kingdom and teaching about how the kingdom grows. What lessons can we learn about evangelism both from his example and from his teaching?

# 6
# Desperate Straits

## *Mark 4:35—6:6*

D on't be afraid; just believe." These words may ring rather hollow when we, and not someone else, face a fearful or life-threatening situation. Yet in the face of real danger we discover just how much faith we have.

In this study we find a number of different people in desperate straits. Their experiences with Jesus can help us to trust him with the fearful areas of our own lives.

**1.** Fear can be a very powerful emotion. What kinds of fear keep you from doing some things you think you should?

**2.** Read Mark 4:35—5:20. In the first incident the disciples are quite naturally afraid of the storm and disturbed that Jesus seems not to be concerned about their drowning. Once Jesus calms the storm, however, they are still terrified. How does their fear after the storm differ from their previous fears?

**3.** Who all in the next incident are afraid and why (5:1-20)?

**4.** How do these fears compare with those in the previous incident?

**5.** Many people find it hard to understand why Jesus allowed the demons to destroy the pigs. It could have been to prevent a violent exit from the man or to show him visibly that he was now free. Even if we can't pin down exactly why Jesus allowed this, what does the fate of the pigs show about what the demons were trying to do to the man?

What does this show about the value Jesus places on the man?

**6.** At the end of this incident Jesus seems to reverse strategy. For the first time he tells someone to go and tell others about his healing. How is this man different from the others? (See 1:21-26; 1:40-45; 3:7-12.)

**7.** Read Mark 5:21—6:6. In 5:21-43 two stories are woven together—that of Jairus's daughter and the woman with a hemorrhage. What sorts of fears are involved in these two incidents?

**8.** The word *fear* doesn't appear in the account of Jesus' return to his hometown, yet a kind of fear is evident here as well. What are the people afraid of?

**9.** Which of the different kinds of fear that have been described in these incidents might we label as *good* fears and which as *bad?*

**10.** What are the relationships between fear and faith in each of these incidents?

**11.** What keeps you from turning your fears into faith?

**12.** Study two (Mark 1:14-39) emphasized Jesus' authority over a similar array of life's experiences. What new dimensions of Jesus' authority are shown here?

How can this authority calm your fears and strengthen your faith?

**13.** Thinking back to the parable of the sower, what kinds of soil can you find in this passage?

# 7
# Understanding the Loaves

## *Mark 6:6-52*

Burnout is all too common an experience among Christians today. One of its most disastrous consequences is a hardened heart that keeps us from being refreshed by our Lord. In this study we see the disciples suffering from burnout and catch a vision of how Jesus can help us to counteract its effects. The passage we are focusing on is especially rich in Old Testament allusions. See if you can spot some of these allusions.

**1.** Do you ever feel that your Bible study is boring, your prayers are pathetic, your ministry is miserable and your spiritual life is lifeless? Explain.

**2.** Read Mark 6:6-52. What do Jesus' instructions to the Twelve tell us about the kind of ministry they were to have (vv. 6-13)?

**3.** What kind of man was Herod (vv. 14-29)?

**4.** In terms of the parable of the sower, what kind of soil was he?

**5.** This flashback to the execution of John the Baptist interrupts the account of Jesus' sending out the Twelve to preach and heal. Why do you suppose Mark recounts it here?

**6.** What differences are there between Jesus' approach to the crowd and that of his disciples (vv. 30-44)?

**7.** When has tiredness blunted your desire to care for others?

**8.** Jesus and Herod, the two kings in this passage, both serve banquets. Compare the two.

**9.** Imagine yourself as one of the disciples in the boat (vv. 45-52). How would you respond to seeing Jesus walking on the water?

**10.** What should the disciples have understood about the loaves (v. 52)?

**11.** Mark tells us that the disciples failed to understand the loaves because their hearts were hardened. What all seems to have led to this hardness of heart?

**12.** Recognizing the contributing factors, what steps can we take to counteract burnout and hardened hearts?

# 8
# Violating Tradition
## *Mark 6:53—7:37*

All of us are influenced by traditions of one sort or another—even those of us who *by tradition* don't put much stock in them! But at what point do traditions lose their value or even become counterproductive? When do religious practices become a substitute for really obeying God?

In this study Jesus has some rather harsh words for the Pharisees and the traditions they choose to observe. See if you can discover the reason for his anger.

**1.** What religious traditions influence your life? Is that influence good or bad? Explain.

**2.** Read Mark 6:53—7:37. At the end of chapter 6 we see that as Jesus moves through the marketplace he goes about healing the sick. What by contrast happens to the Pharisees as they travel through the marketplace (7:1-4)?

**3.** What specific complaints does Jesus raise against the Pharisees' approach to tradition (vv. 6-13)?

**4.** What sorts of traditions do we observe today that get in the way of really honoring God?

**5.** How does Jesus' view of becoming "unclean" differ from that of the Pharisees (vv. 14-23)?

**6.** In what ways do we sometimes emphasize appearance over internal reality?

**7.** Many of the traditions of the elders were embellishments on the Old Testament ceremonial law. Thus the observance of the law and the traditions served to distinguish Jews from Gentiles. How does Jesus' standard of uncleanness cut across the Jew-Gentile distinctions?

**8.** Jesus responds to the Syrophoenician woman's request with a miniparable about children, bread and dogs (vv. 24-27). What is he actually saying?

**9.** What evidence is there that the woman has understood Jesus' point (vv. 28-30)?

**10.** The healing of the deaf man takes place in the Decapolis where Jesus has exorcised the demons from the Gerasene man at the tombs (5:1-20). How do the events here demonstrate that man's success in telling about what Jesus had done for him (vv. 31-37)?

**11.** What practical purposes do you think were served by Jesus' putting his fingers into the deaf man's ears and touching his tongue?

**12.** Throughout Mark's Gospel physical ailments are seen to have spiritual counterparts. The deaf man in this account is obviously someone who quite literally has ears but is unable to hear or speak properly. In this chapter and the previous one, what different people exhibit symptoms of *spiritual* deafness?

How does their deafness affect the kinds of things they say?

**13.** Now, as then, those who are spiritually deaf—whether through hardness of heart or through substituting traditions for true obedience—can be healed by Jesus. Pray for yourself and others who need Jesus' healing touch.

# 9
# Who Do You Say I Am?

## *Mark 8:1—9:1*

W
ho do you say I am?" The whole Gospel of Mark so far has been supplying evidence for answering this question. It's a question Jesus asks each of us, and the answer we give ultimately determines our destiny. But our answer involves more than what we say with our lips. Our real answer is to be found in the way we live our lives.

C. S. Lewis made famous a set of contemporary alternative responses to Jesus' question—legend, liar, lunatic or Lord? What is your response?

**1.** Read Mark 8:1—9:1. Why do you suppose the disciples, having witnessed the feeding of the 5,000, have such a hard time believing Jesus can supply the needs of 4,000 here (8:1-13)?

**2.** When have you acted similarly, not expecting God to work just after he has met a need in your life?

**3.** What details in Mark's account stress the adequacy of Jesus' ability to meet the people's needs?

**4.** In verse 12 Jesus says he will give no sign to this generation. What do you think he means in light of the many miraculous signs and healings he has already performed, not to mention his coming death and resurrection?

**5.** What is the yeast of the Pharisees and Herod (v. 15)? (For clues, look back to 6:14-29 and 7:1-23.)

**6.** What do the disciples fail to understand in verses 14-21 and why?

**7.** What unusual thing happens while Jesus is curing the blind man (vv. 22-26)?

**8.** In response to Jesus' question of who people are saying he is, the disciples tell him John the Baptist, Elijah or one of the prophets (vv. 27-30). Why would people think Jesus was any one of these?

**9.** What different answers do people today give regarding who Jesus is?

**10.** Right after Peter acknowledges Jesus to be the Christ, Jesus begins to explain what must happen to him. Why do you suppose Peter reacts so strongly to what Jesus has said?

**11.** Why does Jesus respond to Peter so harshly?

**12.** How is Peter like the blind man in verses 22-26?

**13.** What does Jesus say it means to acknowledge him as the Christ and to follow him?

**14.** Is your life characterized more by seeking to lose your life or to save it? Explain.

**15.** Ask Jesus to help you to see more clearly those areas where you are not yet following him.

# 10
# Review
## *Mark 1—8*

The truth about Jesus has progressively unfolded in Mark 1—8. With Peter's confession in 8:29 we reach not only the midpoint but also a key turning point in Mark's Gospel. For this reason it is especially useful to review some of the key themes developed thus far.

**1.** What are some of the things Mark has most emphasized about Jesus?

**2.** What key things have been revealed about his kingdom?

**3.** Go back through each study so far and retitle it to show how it fits in with the kingdom theme. For example, study one could be titled "The Coming of the Promised King."

**4.** How can we make the message of the king and his kingdom a more vital part of our proclaiming the good news?

**5.** What have we observed about Jesus as a communicator of the gospel?

**6.** How can this improve the way we communicate the gospel?

**7.** Throughout the early chapters of Mark, Jesus seems cautious about revealing his identity too quickly. Why do you think this is so?

**8.** In the parable of the sower we first confront the problem of hearing. Jesus talks about the failure of the path, the rocky soil and the thorn-infested soil to produce fruit. As we move on we begin to see that even the disciples have difficulty hearing and seeing because their hearts are hardened. How is this problem—the hardened heart, the blind eyes and the deaf ears—to be solved?

**9.** What are some areas where you have begun to see more clearly and to hear with a more responsive heart?

# Part 2
# Why Did Jesus Come?

*Mark 9—16*

# 1
# Suffering and Glory
## Mark 9:2-32

I n a famous short story, the main character is given the choice of opening one of two doors. Behind one is a beautiful maiden; behind the other, a ferocious tiger. It is easy to identify with the hero of the story, hoping for joy rather than suffering, pleasure rather than pain. But what if we cannot have one without the other?

This passage examines the relationship between suffering and glory, human weakness and divine power.

**1.** Read Mark 9:2-32. The transfiguration occurs six days after Jesus' statement, "I tell you the truth, some who are standing here will not taste death before they see the kingdom of God come with power" (9:1). What connection do you see between the transfiguration and Jesus' promise?

**2.** What is the significance of the presence of Elijah and Moses with Jesus on the mount?

**3.** In this account God's voice is heard for a second time in Mark's Gospel, the first being in 1:11. What purposes are accomplished by God's affirmation here?

**4.** The statement in verse 7, "Listen to him!" probably alludes to Deuteronomy 18:14-22. Explain how we can listen to Jesus today.

**5.** To what events is Jesus referring when he says, "Elijah has come and they have done to him everything they wished, just as it is written about him" (v. 13)?

**6.** Elijah's return was expected to immediately precede the inauguration of the glorious messianic kingdom (Mal 4:5). Yet how is what happened to him (v. 13) a pattern for what must also happen to Jesus (vv. 9, 12) and to us?

**7.** Jesus descends the mountain and returns to his other disciples only to find them in hot debate with the teachers of the law over their failure to exorcise a young boy robbed of speech (vv. 14-18). Why do you suppose Jesus is so harsh in verse 19?

**8.** Think back to the leper in chapter 1. How is the father's request in verse 22 similar to and yet different from the leper's request in 1:40?

**9.** Which do you struggle with more—believing that Jesus *can* or that he *wants* to answer your prayers? Explain.

**10.** How can the dialog between Jesus and the man encourage you when your faith is weak?

**11.** At the end of this account, Jesus again tells his disciples about his death and resurrection (vv. 30-32). Why do you suppose the disciples failed to understand what he meant?

**12.** What details in the account of the boy's healing parallel those in Jesus' prediction of his coming suffering and victory?

**13.** How can this passage encourage us in the midst of pain and suffering?

# 2
# The First
# and the Last
## *Mark 9:33-50*

All of us, I imagine, struggle with the question of status and identity within a group. Where do I fit? How important am I to this group? Who is on our side? Who isn't? In this study we find out how Jesus turns conventional wisdom about status and group identity on its ear.

**1.** How would you define success? Would you say you've achieved it?

**2.** Read Mark 9:33-50. In verses 33-37, what is Jesus trying to get across to the disciples?

**3.** Thinking back through all the Gospel of Mark to this point, how have we seen this principle of the first and the last in action?

**4.** Why is a child so appropriate an illustration for Jesus' point?

**5.** What attitudes that we all share motivate John's remarks in verse 38?

**6.** What perspective governs Jesus' response to John in verses 39-41?

**7.** What further rebuke to John is given in verses 42-50?

**8.** How are Jesus' attitudes about greatness and personal worth radically different from attitudes we often adopt from society?

**9.** Christian history has known some individuals to take Jesus' words in verses 43-47 quite literally. Why is cutting off a hand or foot or plucking out an eye not radical enough a way to deal with sin?

**10.** Verse 49 is somewhat of a mixed metaphor, but fire has been used as an image in verses 42-48. Taking a cue from 42-48, what do you think it means to be "salted with fire"?

**11.** If salt is connected with fire as an image of judgment, what do you think having salt in yourself might mean?

How would that contribute to peace?

**12.** What individuals or groups are we tempted to silence because they are not one of us?

**13.** Does this mean we shouldn't oppose anyone, or does Jesus give limits?

**14.** What attitudes and actions does this passage suggest should govern our relationships with rival individuals or groups who act in Jesus' name?

# 3
# Divorce, Children and Eternal Life

## *Mark 10:1-31*

For many of us preachin' becomes meddlin' when it impinges on how we live. But Jesus and the New Testament, like the Old Testament before them, never allow religion to be divorced from family life and social relationships. This passage exposes some of the ways the gospel ought to transform some of these areas of our life.

**1.** What do you think of divorce?

**2.** Read Mark 10:1-31. What differences in approach to the question of divorce seem evident between Jesus and the Pharisees?

**3.** On the basis of verses 6-9, some Christian churches have refused to recognize divorce even when a couple has obtained a civil dissolution of their marriage. Do you think this is the intent of Jesus' statement? Why or why not?

**4.** In a culture which granted far more freedom to men than to women, what significant further statements on divorce does Jesus make in verses 11-12?

**5.** In verses 13-16 we find that Jesus has used a child or children for the second time to illustrate a spiritual principle. What does it mean to receive the kingdom like a little child?

**6.** What kind of answer does the rich man expect from Jesus in response to his question (v. 17)?

**7.** What kind of answer does Jesus actually give him (vv. 18-21)?

**8.** Why is it so hard for the rich to enter the kingdom (vv. 22-27)?

**9.** What obstacles were or are hardest for you to overcome in entering the kingdom?

What evidence has there been of God's help in your overcoming these obstacles?

**10.** How have the Pharisees (vv. 2-9) and the rich man (vv. 17-25) failed to receive the kingdom like a child (v. 15)?

**11.** In what areas of your life do you most need to express more childlike faith in God?

**12.** What does Peter seem to be getting at by his comments in verse 28?

**13.** How does Jesus reassure Peter?

**14.** What somber note does Jesus strike in the midst of his reassurance?

**15.** How have you experienced the truth of Jesus' words here?

# 4
# Blindness and Sight

## *Mark 10:32-52*

The blind sometimes have uncanny "sight," and the deaf sometimes "hear" what others miss. Spiritual insight and alertness arise from the heart rather than from status or position. In this passage Mark seems to delight in the irony of a blind man who perceives what the sighted cannot see.

**1.** What do you think are some of the privileges and responsibilities of a leader?

**2.** Read Mark 10:32-52. In verses 32-34, Jesus predicts his death for a third time. Compare this prediction with the previous two (8:31; 9:31).

**3.** Given what Jesus has just said, what is ironic about James and John's request (vv. 35-37)?

**4.** What seems to motivate James and John's request?


Why do you think they go about asking the way they do?


---

**5.** What does Jesus mean by the cup he is to drink and the baptism he is to be baptized with (vv. 38-39)?


---

**6.** When the other ten apostles hear about this status request, they become indignant. In response, what principle does Jesus bring out again (see 9:35 and 10:31)?


---

**7.** What new motivation for service is found in verse 45?


---

**8.** How can your life better conform to Jesus' view of greatness? (Consider what motivates your actions as well as what you do.)


---

**9.** From the brief account in verses 46-52, what kind of man does Bartimaeus seem to be?

**10.** Why do you suppose Jesus asked Bartimaeus what he wanted him to do for him?

**11.** Once Jesus heals him, Bartimaeus sets out to follow Jesus along the road. What road is Jesus on (10:33-34; 11:1)?

**12.** What might it mean for Bartimaeus to be on this road (10:32-34)?

**13.** What has Bartimaeus seen that the disciples have not?

**14.** Jesus is indeed on the road to glory, but that road will not bypass Jerusalem. Self-sacrifice and service mark the way. What are some present opportunities for you to follow him?

What may be some of the costs?

# 5
# Palm Sunday

## *Mark 11:1-25*

The trouble with righteous anger is that it is so much easier to be angry than righteous. But it is possible to be both, as Jesus well illustrates in this passage. He also suggests that even righteous anger must be joined with prayer and forgiveness. This passage provides an example of how our emotions and attitudes can work toward God's purposes instead of against them.

**1.** How would you define righteous anger? Why do we so seldom express it?

**2.** Read Mark 11:1-25. What progression of moods do you see in this passage?

**3.** What significant event is taking place in verses 1-11?

**4.** In what ways is the significance of Jesus' entry into Jerusalem reinforced?

**5.** Why is Jesus so angry with what is taking place in the temple (vv. 15-17)?

**6.** Are there similar activities or attitudes in your church or fellowship which get in the way of God's purposes?

What can you do to help eliminate them?

**7.** Why do you suppose Mark has sandwiched this account of Jesus' clearing out of the temple within that of the cursing of the fig tree?

What kind of fruit was Jesus looking for in Israel?

**8.** Many people believe they will escape the judgment of God simply because they are religious. How can this passage serve as a warning to them and to us?

**9.** What does Jesus teach us about prayer in verses 23-25?


**10.** Jesus may have had a more specific meaning in verse 23. As he spoke these words the Mount of Olives would have been in view. Zechariah prophesied that the Lord will one day return to the Mount of Olives to judge his enemies and to establish his kingdom. As his feet touch the Mount, it will move out of the way. If praying to move mountains is praying for the day of God's judgment, why is it important to pray with the attitude Jesus describes in verse 25?


**11.** Thinking back to your response to question 6, are there any people you need to forgive as well as to rebuke?


Is there anything else you need to do to be reconciled to this person or persons? If so, how and when will you do it?


**12.** Respond to this passage in prayer, praising the King of peace and asking that his kingdom might be established.

# 6
# Tempting Questions

## Mark 11:27—12:27

Some people ask questions because they want to know the answers. Others take malicious delight in posing unanswerable questions or in trying to trip up an opponent. Jesus often asked questions to get his hearers to think deeply for themselves. Learning to look behind questions to motives and learning to pose effective questions can help us all to be better evangelists and servants. As you read Mark 11:27—12:27, look for the motives behind the questions that are asked.

**1.** In verse 27 the chief priests, the elders and the teachers of the law come asking a seemingly straightforward question about Jesus' authority. What does Jesus' reply and the subsequent discussion reveal about their motives?

**2.** Why doesn't Jesus answer them?

**3.** Are there times when we shouldn't answer questioners? Explain.

**4.** The parable of the tenants is rich in meaning, especially in light of its allusion to Isaiah's Song of the Vineyard (Is 5:1-7). If the tenants are Israel and its religious leaders, who are the owner, the servants and the son?

**5.** How are these religious leaders about to fulfill the scripture Jesus cites in verses 10-11?

**6.** A common enemy can often draw together people who are not otherwise on good terms. In verses 13-17 we find Herodians (supporters of the puppet monarchy) and the Pharisees (ardent nationalists and opponents of Roman rule) joining forces. How does the question they pose to Jesus reflect their conflicting interests?

**7.** Jesus not only avoids their trap by his answer, he also succeeds in establishing an important principle. What sorts of things are rightfully Caesar's (the government's) and what are God's?

**8.** The Sadducees differed from their Jewish contemporaries because they rejected the idea of resurrection. What motives lie behind their question to Jesus (vv. 18-23)?

**9.** How do the Sadducees display ignorance of the Scriptures and the power of God?

**10.** How are you experiencing the truth of the Scriptures and the power of God?

**11.** How can we get to know the Scriptures and the power of God better?

**12.** How is Jesus' response from Scripture particularly appropriate for the Sadducees who accepted only the authority of the Pentateuch?

**13.** As we seek to share the good news of Christ and his kingdom, we will meet people with a wide variety of questions and motives. What can we learn about answering and asking questions from this passage?

# 7
# An End to Questions

## *Mark 12:28-44*

People are motivated by many things—ambition, money, power, recognition, the desire to please God. What motivates your daily life and future plans?

In this passage Jesus encounters or comments on a variety of people whose lives are governed by different goals. In so doing he exposes our own motivations to his searching glance.

**1.** Read Mark 12:28-44. Like the chief priests, elders, Pharisees and Sadducees of 11:27—12:27, another teacher of the law comes to Jesus with a pointed question (v. 28). What evidence is there that he is not out to trap Jesus?

**2.** Though Jesus is only asked for one commandment (Deut 6:4-5), in good rabbinic fashion he responds by adding a second to his reply (Lev 19:18). What relationship does this second commandment bear to the first?

**3.** The teacher not only endorses Jesus' answer, he takes it a step further. What are some contemporary examples of burnt offerings and sacrifices?


**4.** If you were to evaluate your daily activities on the basis of love for God and neighbor, how would you fare? Explain.


**5.** What steps can you take to make the love of God and love of neighbor a higher priority in your life?


**6.** How has Jesus succeeded in silencing his questioners? (Look back over 11:27—12:34 to answer this.)


**7.** To a Jew in Jesus' day a descendant was always inferior to an ancestor. A son might call his father or grandfather "lord" but never vice versa. How *can* Christ be both David's Lord and his descendant?


**8.** What does it mean for us to call Jesus "Lord"?

**9.** What warning to us is present in Jesus' cautions about the teachers of the law (vv. 38-40)?

**10.** In contrast to the teachers of the law and the rich, what motivates the widow's religious behavior?

**11.** How does she fulfill the great commandment?

**12.** What implications does this example have for our giving to the Lord's work?

**13.** Read Malachi 3:1-5. In what ways has Jesus been fulfilling this prophecy in chapters 11—12 of Mark's Gospel?

# 8
# Keep Watch

## *Mark 13:1-37*

Waiting for Christmas can keep some children excited and on their best behavior for weeks. But what if Christmas never came? To many of us the Second Coming may seem like a Christmas that never comes. In this passage, Jesus answers some questions about the future, both near and far off, but above all he encourages an attitude we all need to develop.

**1.** Why do you think so many of us have such a fascination with the future?

**2.** Read Mark 13:1-37. From the context what are Peter, James, John and Andrew asking about in verse 4?

**3.** Jesus doesn't seem to answer their question directly, at least not at first. What is he concerned about?

**4.** How would Jesus' warnings and encouragements (vv. 5-13) have helped the disciples in the early years of the church?


**5.** What relevance do these warnings and encouragements have for us today?


**6.** Christians have sometimes disagreed about how to interpret Jesus' words in verses 14-23. Some think Jesus is talking about the destruction of the temple in A.D. 70 and the events leading up to that. Others think these events are still future. Perhaps both views are correct. What evidence is there to support each view?


**7.** What does Jesus say about God's work in the midst of all this turmoil?


**8.** How is the distress described in verses 24-27 different from that described in verses 5-23?


**9.** How would verses 26-27 encourage those who have experienced the distress preceding Jesus' return?

**10.** Six times Jesus warns his disciples to "watch, be on guard" (vv. 5, 9, 23, 33, 35, 37). Why?

**11.** Many people throughout the ages have tried to make precise predictions about the return of Jesus. How does watching as Jesus urges differ from making such predictions?

**12.** In what practical ways can we be alert for Jesus' return?

# 9
# The Betrayer Approaches

## *Mark 14:1-42*

Lf you've ever caught yourself yawning at a critical moment or felt spiritually asleep when the Lord was calling you to a task, you'll have little difficulty in empathizing with the disciples in this account. We enter clearly now into the last few days of Jesus' earthly ministry. The mood is somber as more and more people begin to fail and desert him. Try to empathize with Jesus as you read Mark 14:1-42.

**1.** Read Mark 14:1-42. What different motives are present in the conflict that arises at the home of Simon the Leper?

**2.** What legitimate concerns do the objectors raise?

How might Jesus' own teaching have prompted their response?

**3.** The woman's act is in one sense an act of worship. What light, if any, does this incident shed on the competing claims for beauty in worship and concern for the poor?

**4.** During the Passover feast Jesus tells the Twelve that one of them will betray him. What do you think they were feeling as they responded to his announcement (v. 19)?

**5.** Few words have spawned as much debate regarding their meaning as those Jesus spoke in verses 22-24. Regardless of how literally we take them, what are the bread and cup of the Lord's Supper to symbolize for us?

**6.** In verse 27 Jesus predicts that his disciples will desert him under pressure. How do you empathize or fail to empathize with Peter's assertions in verses 29-31?

**7.** Many people question whether the *only* way to God is through Jesus and his death on the cross. Edith Schaeffer has suggested that this is the question Jesus himself wrestled with in Gethsemane (vv. 35-36). What conclusion did he reach?

How might this passage help those who struggle with the question of whether Jesus is the only way to God?

**8.** In verse 34 and again in verse 38, Jesus encourages the disciples to watch and pray so that they not fall into temptation. What particular temptations were they about to face?

How might prayer have changed the outcome?

**9.** How can these same exhortations make the difference in your own life between resisting or falling into temptation?

**10.** Have you ever felt like the disciples must have felt in verse 40? Explain.

**11.** What consolation and encouragement can you draw from the disciples' experience?

# 10
# Betrayed!

### *Mark 14:43-72*

The persecution of enemies is one thing, the abandonment of friends another. In this study we find Jesus not only betrayed by one of his disciples but abandoned by all the others and ruefully denied by one of his closest friends. All this added to the cruel and unlawful treatment by the Sanhedrin. This account reveals how intense pressures can test the quality of our discipleship.

**1.** What does being loyal to a friend mean to you?

**2.** Read Mark 14:43-72. Several of the main characters in this passage act with mixed motives. What mixed motives may have inspired Judas's words and action of betrayal (vv. 43-45)?

**3.** How does Jesus respond to his betrayal?

**4.** The unnamed young man seems symbolic of all Jesus' followers. How does his predicament reflect Jesus' warnings about the cost of discipleship (8:34-38)?

**5.** What aspects of Jesus' trial before the Sanhedrin does Mark emphasize?

**6.** Up until this point Jesus has regularly disguised his identity, but in verse 62 he openly confesses his identity as the Christ. Why do you think he does this now?

**7.** On what charge is Jesus finally condemned?

**8.** How is this charge both justifiable and unjustifiable?

**9.** How is Jesus, in contrast to his disciples, an example of the kind of discipleship he desires in us (vv. 55-65)?

**10.** What mix of motives brings Peter into the high priest's courtyard yet keeps him from acknowledging his relationship to Jesus (vv. 66-72)?

**11.** How are your motives mixed in following Jesus?

**12.** How is Judas's betrayal of Jesus different from Peter's?

**13.** In what circumstances are you most tempted to be ashamed of Jesus or to deny him?

**14.** What warnings and encouragement can you draw from Peter's experience?

# 11
# Victory Snatched from Defeat
## *Mark 15:1—16:8*

True greatness, Jesus taught, is found in being a servant: "Whoever wants to be first must be slave of all. For even the Son of Man did not come to be served, but to serve, and to give his life as a ransom for many." Recorded here is the vivid testimony to Jesus' greatness and glory. As you read 15:1—16:8, look for incentives to imitate his gospel-sharing servant life.

**1.** What kind of man is Pilate (vv. 1-15)?

**2.** What evidence is there that he wants to do what is right?

**3.** What keeps him from doing what is right?

**4.** How can we keep from succumbing to the same temptation?

**5.** In what sense is Barrabas a stand-in for every believer?

**6.** The wine mixed with myrrh offered to Jesus would have had a narcotic effect. Why does Jesus refuse it? (See 10:38; 14:25, 36.)

**7.** What ironies are present in the charges and jeers directed toward Jesus on the cross (vv. 25-32)?

**8.** In verse 34 Jesus quotes the first verse of Psalm 22. What other aspects of this psalm is Jesus experiencing?

**9.** In what ways is the centurion's confession a climax to the whole of Mark's Gospel? (Compare 15:38-39 with 1:1, 10-11; 8:28-30.)

**10.** Why do you think it was Joseph and the women who had followed Jesus, and not the eleven, who were present when Jesus died and his body needed a tomb?

**11.** Why is it significant that Peter is mentioned by name in verse 7?

**12.** What reassurance can we draw from the Lord's evident forgiveness of Peter (see 3:28)?

**13.** The earliest and best manuscripts of Mark's Gospel end at verse 8. Nearly all scholars agree that if Mark did not end his work here, we have lost what he wrote (vv. 9-20 were clearly written by someone else). While some still hold that the original ending has been lost, a growing number of scholars believe Mark intended to end with verse 8 as it is. How is verse 8 an appropriate ending to the gospel story?

**14.** How can this passage reinforce our commitment to sharing the good news of Christ with others?

# 12
# Review

## *Mark 9—16*

D o you bring in a lamp to put it under a bowl or a bed? Instead, don't you put it on its stand? For whatever is hidden is meant to be disclosed, and whatever is concealed is meant to be brought out into the open. If anyone has ears to hear, let him hear."

New light brings new responsibility. Now that you have concluded your study of Mark, how will your life be different? This final study reviews some of the central themes of Mark's Gospel and reminds us of how they are to affect our lives.

**1.** What have you learned about Mark as a writer and an evangelist?

**2.** How has your understanding of the gospel and the kingdom been enriched?

**3.** The disciples' performance in this half of Mark's Gospel has been almost entirely marked by failure (9:18-19; 10:35-45; 14:32-42, 43-52, 66-72). Review the specific instances of failure and then explain why Mark may have drawn so much attention to them.

What can we learn from this?

**4.** Many scholars believe one of Mark's purposes in writing his account of Jesus' ministry was to counteract a misconception about Jesus himself and the Christian life.[1] Some Christians tended to emphasize Jesus as a glorious, otherworldly figure to the exclusion of his humanity and suffering. As a result they expected to be spared suffering in this life and to quickly join Jesus in the glories of heaven. Unfortunately, many Christians today share this view of the Christian life. How does Mark systematically undercut this view? (Be sure to consider the themes of following Christ, the cost of discipleship and the road to glory.)

**5.** Where in Mark's account is Jesus' glory most prominently displayed? Give reasons to support your answer.

**6.** How might the cross fulfill Jesus words in 9:1, at least in part?

---

**7.** If the path to glory is marked by discipline, suffering and servanthood, how will your life need to change?

How will your sharing of the gospel need to change?

---

**8.** What did you appreciate most about your study of Mark?

---

[1]See, for example, Ralph Martin, *Mark: The Evangelist and Theologian* (Grand Rapids, Mich.: Zondervan, 1972).

# Leader's Notes

Leading a Bible discussion can be an enjoyable and rewarding experience. But it can also be *scary*—especially if you've never done it before. If this is your feeling, you're in good company. When God asked Moses to lead the Israelites out of Egypt, he replied, "O Lord, please send someone else to do it!" (Ex 4:13).

When Solomon became king of Israel, he felt the task was far beyond his abilities. "I am only a little child and do not know how to carry out my duties. . . . Who is able to govern this great people of yours?" (1 Kings 3:7, 9).

When God called Jeremiah to be a prophet, he replied, "Ah, Sovereign LORD, . . . I do not know how to speak; I am only a child" (Jer 1:6).

The list goes on. The apostles were "unschooled, ordinary men" (Acts 4:13). Timothy was young, frail and frightened. Paul's "thorn in the flesh" made him feel weak. But God's response to all of his servants—including you—is essentially the same: "My grace is sufficient for you" (2 Cor 12:9). Relax. God helped these people in spite of their weaknesses, and he can help you in spite of your feelings of inadequacy.

There is another reason why you should feel encouraged. Leading a Bible discussion is not difficult if you follow certain guidelines. You don't need to be an expert on the Bible or a trained teacher. The suggestions listed below should enable you to effectively and enjoyably fulfill your role as leader.

## Preparing to Lead

**1.** Ask God to help you understand and apply the passage to your own life. Unless this happens, you will not be prepared to lead others. Pray too for the various members of the group. Ask God to give you an enjoyable and profitable time together studying his Word.

**2.** As you begin each study, read and reread the assigned Bible passage to familiarize yourself with what the author is saying. In the case of book studies, you may want to read through the entire book prior to the first study. This will give you a helpful overview of its contents.

**3.** This study guide is based on the New International Version of the Bible. It will help you and the group if you use this translation as the basis for your study and discussion. Encourage others to use the NIV also, but allow them the freedom to use whatever translation they prefer.

**4.** Carefully work through each question in the study. Spend time in meditation and reflection as you formulate your answers.

**5.** Write your answers in the space provided in the study guide. This will help you to express your understanding of the passage clearly.

**6.** It might help you to have a Bible dictionary handy. Use it to look up any unfamiliar words, names or places. (For additional help on how to study a passage, see chapter five of *Leading Bible Discussions,* IVP.)

**7.** Once you have finished your own study of the passage, familiarize yourself with the leader's notes for the study you are leading. These are designed to help you in several ways. First, they tell you the purpose the study guide author had in mind while writing the study. Take time to think through how the study questions work together to accomplish that purpose. Second, the notes provide you with additional background information or comments on some of the questions. This information can be useful if people have difficulty understanding or answering a question. Third, the leader's notes can alert you to potential problems you may encounter during the study.

**8.** If you wish to remind yourself of anything mentioned in the leader's notes, make a note to yourself below that question in the study.

## Leading the Study

**1.** Begin the study on time. Unless you are leading an evangelistic Bible study, open with prayer, asking God to help you to understand and apply the passage.

**2.** Be sure that everyone in your group has a study guide. Encourage them to prepare beforehand for each discussion by working through the questions in the guide.

**3.** At the beginning of your first time together, explain that these studies are meant to be discussions not lectures. Encourage the members of the group to participate. However, do not put pressure on those who may be hesitant to speak during the first few sessions.

**4.** Read the introductory paragraph at the beginning of the discussion. This will orient the group to the passage being studied.

**5.** Read the passage aloud if you are studying one chapter or less. You may choose to do this yourself, or someone else may read if he or she has been asked to do so prior to the study. Longer passages may occasionally be read in parts at different times during the study. Some studies may cover several chapters. In such cases reading aloud would probably take too much time, so the group members should simply read the assigned passages prior to the study.

**6.** As you begin to ask the questions in the guide, keep several things in mind. First, the questions are designed to be used just as they are written. If you wish, you may simply read them aloud to the group. Or you may prefer to express them in your own words. However, unnecessary rewording of the questions is not recommended.

Second, the questions are intended to guide the group toward understanding and applying the *main idea* of the passage. The author of the guide has stated his or her view of this central idea in the *purpose* of the study in the leader's notes. You should try to understand how the passage expresses this idea and how the study questions work together to lead the group in that direction.

There may be times when it is appropriate to deviate from the study guide. For example, a question may have already been answered. If so, move on to the next question. Or someone may raise an important question not covered in the guide. Take time to discuss it! The important thing is to use discretion. There may be many routes you can travel to reach the goal of the study. But the easiest route is usually the one the author has suggested.

**7.** Avoid answering your own questions. If necessary, repeat or rephrase them until they are clearly understood. An eager group quickly becomes passive and silent if they think the leader will do most of the talking.

**8.** Don't be afraid of silence. People may need time to think about the question before formulating their answers.

**9.** Don't be content with just one answer. Ask, "What do the rest of you think?" or "Anything else?" until several people have given answers to the question.

**10.** Acknowledge all contributions. Try to be affirming whenever possible. Never reject an answer. If it is clearly wrong, ask, "Which verse led you to that conclusion?" or again, "What do the rest of you think?"

**11.** Don't expect every answer to be addressed to you, even though this will probably happen at first. As group members become more at ease, they will begin to truly interact with each other. This is one sign of a healthy discussion.

**12.** Don't be afraid of controversy. It can be very stimulating. If you don't resolve an issue completely, don't be frustrated. Move on and keep it in mind for later. A subsequent study may solve the problem.

**13.** Stick to the passage under consideration. It should be the source for answering the questions. Discourage the group from unnecessary cross-referencing. Likewise, stick to the subject and avoid going off on tangents.

**14.** Periodically summarize what the *group* has said about the passage. This helps to draw together the various ideas mentioned and gives continuity to the study. But don't preach.

**15.** Conclude your time together with conversational prayer. Be sure to ask God's help to apply those things which you learned in the study.

**16.** End on time.

Many more suggestions and helps are found in *Leading Bible Discussions* (IVP). Reading and studying through that would be well worth your time.

## Components of Small Groups

A healthy small group should do more than study the Bible. There are four components you should consider as you structure your time together.

*Nurture.* Being a part of a small group should be a nurturing and edifying experience. You should grow in your knowledge and love of God and each other. If we are to properly love God, we must know and keep his commandments (Jn 14:15). That is why Bible study should be a foundational part of your small group. But you can be nurtured by other things as well. You can memorize Scripture, read and discuss a book, or occasionally listen to a tape of a good speaker.

*Community.* Most people have a need for close friendships. Your small group can be an excellent place to cultivate such relationships. Allow time for informal interaction before and after the study. Have a time of sharing during the meeting. Do fun things together as a group, such as a potluck supper or a picnic. Have someone bring refreshments to the meeting. Be creative!

*Worship.* A portion of your time together can be spent in worship and prayer. Praise God together for who he is. Thank him for what he has done and is doing in your lives and in the world. Pray for each other's needs. Ask God to help you to apply what you have learned. Sing hymns together.

*Mission.* Many small groups decide to work together in some form of outreach. This can be a practical way of applying what you have learned. You can host a series of evangelistic discussions for your friends or neighbors. You can visit people at a home for the elderly. Help a widow with cleaning or repair jobs around her home. Such projects can have a transforming influence on your group.

For a detailed discussion of the nature and function of small groups, read *Small Group Leaders' Handbook* or *Good Things Come in Small Groups* (both from IVP).

## The Big Picture

In any set of studies covering a whole book like Mark, there is an inevitable trade-off between giving attention to details and getting the big picture. If these studies err on one side or the other, they err on the side of trying to see the big picture. Thus some passages may seem a little long, but they have a unified theme. And from time to time you will find questions which ask you to tie together observations from previous studies.

I think the effort to see the gospel as a whole, rather than as a set of isolated units, will be richly rewarding. But it will require discipline on the part of leader and group members together to press on and not get bogged down in details.

## Part 1: Who Is Jesus?
## Study 1. Gospel Beginnings. Mark 1:1-13.

*Purpose:* To see how the gospel is rooted in history and prophecy.

**Question 1.** Almost every study begins with an "approach" question, which is meant to be asked *before* the passage is read. These questions are important for several reasons.

First, they help the group to warm up to each other. No matter how well a group may know each other or how comfortable they may be with each other, there is always a stiffness that needs to be overcome before people will begin to talk openly. A good question will break the ice.

Second, approach questions get people thinking along the lines of the topic of the study. Most people will have lots of different things going on in their minds (dinner, an important meeting coming up, how to get the car fixed) that will have nothing to do with the study. A creative question will get their attention and draw them into the discussion.

Third, approach questions can reveal where our thoughts or feelings need to be transformed by Scripture. This is why it is especially important *not* to read the passage before the approach question is asked. The passage will tend to color the honest reactions people would otherwise give because they are of course *supposed* to think the way the Bible does. Giving honest responses to various issues before they find out what the Bible says may help them to see where their thoughts or attitudes need to be changed.

This approach question is designed to get the group thinking about how family histories give us a sense of identity and continuity with the past. The rest of the study will look at how Mark roots the gospel in Jewish history and prophecy.

**Question 2.** The idea here is to see that Mark is not a disinterested observer but a committed believer. Encourage the group to think about the significance of each key word or phrase: *beginning, gospel* (good news), *Jesus Christ, the Son of God.* What we learn here Jesus' contemporaries would only have learned gradually through their interaction with him.

**Question 3.** The quotations Mark cites are from Malachi 3:1 and Isaiah 40:3. Some people in your group may be disturbed that both quotations seem to be attributed to Isaiah. Explain, if necessary, that Mark may have attributed both to Isaiah because they both appeared on the same scroll or that he may simply have named the more significant prophet in drawing the two texts together. It was common rabbinic practice in Jesus' day to demonstrate one's knowledge of the Scriptures by drawing together separate but related texts. Notice how Jesus does this with Deuteronomy 6:4-5 and Leviticus 19:18 in Mark 12:30-31.

**Question 4.** Kings about to go on a journey often sent out a messenger to have the way prepared for them. Roads would be straightened, potholes filled in, bumps taken out. Mark draws on this kind of imagery from Isaiah's description of the Lord's coming to reign as king over his people. Numerous Old Testament passages describe God as king and foretell a day when he will reign unopposed over his people and creation.

**Question 6.** For group discussion draw on the general knowledge of the group or summarize for them important aspects of Elijah's ministry. Be sure they notice the description of Elijah in 2 Kings 1:8.

**Question 10.** Though Jesus is without sin, he nevertheless *identifies* with sinners in coming to John for baptism.

## Study 2. Four Portraits. Mark 1:14-39.

*Purpose:* To begin to see Jesus as the servant-king who exercises his authority for the benefit of his subjects.

**Question 2.** Don't spend much time on this question. The goal is to mention a few initial impressions.

**Question 3.** Some people may have trouble answering this question. If so, get them to see the two assertions Jesus makes. Why is it good news that "the time has come" and "the kingdom of God is near"? How does Jesus ask people to respond to this good news?

**Question 4.** Be sure the group sees that the response of these four men shows the success of John the Baptist's ministry of preparation. This is the first of several questions throughout this guide designed to tie together material learned from previous studies.

**Question 5.** Some people may question the reality of demons—aren't they just primitive ways of describing mental and physical ailments? This would be plausible if the Gospels were not so careful about distinguishing physical ills from demon possession. Note that Simon's mother-in-law is not said to

have a demon in the next incident. At least two factors might account for Jesus'
silencing of the demon: (1) a desire to keep his identity hidden for the time
being or (2) a desire not to have his identity revealed by an unreliable source
(would you trust a demon to tell the truth?).

**Question 8.** Be sure the group notices how Jesus' authority is emphasized
by such phrases as "at once" and "without delay." They should also notice
all the areas of life to which Jesus' authority extends: teaching, demons,
disease and people.

**Question 9.** If the group has difficulty answering the question, ask, "In what
ways has the kingdom of God come near the people in these events?" The
key issue here is to see that the kingdom is near because the *king* is present
in the person of Jesus.

**Study 3. A Leper, a Paralytic and a Tax Collector. Mark 1:40—2:17.**
*Purpose:* To see that it is sinners who are invited to enter the kingdom.

**Question 2.** This is not really intended as a question, but you could allow
the group to share their initial impressions concerning the resistance to Jesus.
Don't spend much time on this.

**Question 3.** Be sure that the group, in answering this question or the next,
notices that the way the man feels about himself affects his request. Even
though he seems confident of Jesus' ability to heal, he questions Jesus' willingness to help him.

**Question 4.** Among other things, according to the Law, Jesus would become
ceremonially unclean. He also risked getting the disease.

**Question 5.** Be sure that the group notices that Jesus' stern charges were
oriented toward the man's good and not simply his own convenience. By
fulfilling the requirements of the Law (Lev 14:2-32), the man could be restored to his proper place in the social and religious fabric of society.

**Question 9.** While the NIV puts the word *sinners* in quotation marks, other
versions do not. The point here is that the Pharisees classified as a sinner
anyone who failed to meet their rigid standards. They also failed to recognize
that even the strictest Pharisee might be a sinner in God's eyes.

**Question 10.** Be sure the group notes both the physical and spiritual aspects
of Jesus' work.

**Question 11.** Be sure to explore the social and psychological dimensions
as well as the spiritual.

**Question 12.** If the group has trouble answering, ask, "What would the
Pharisees have to admit about themselves before they would be ready to
follow Jesus?"

**Study 4. Conflict in Galilee. Mark 2:18—3:35.**

*Purpose:* To see the causes of the growing opposition to Jesus and how viewing ourselves as members of God's family can reorient our attitudes toward obedience.

**Question 3.** The group may have difficulty understanding Jesus' two short parables. Encourage them to wrestle with what he says. Why, for instance, would it be inappropriate to fast at a wedding reception? What is Jesus suggesting about himself by talking about new cloth and new wineskins?

**Question 4.** Some members of the group may be troubled to learn that according to 1 Samuel 21 Ahimelech was the high priest when David ate the consecrated bread. Abiathar was Ahimelech's son who later became high priest (1 Sam 22:20). It was surely during his days that the event took place, just as we might say that during President Reagan's days the first atom bomb was exploded and the first trip to the moon was made. There is no need to raise this issue with the group unless one of the members brings it up.

**Question 5.** People may have difficulty seeing how Jesus' words rebuke a lax attitude toward the Sabbath. If so, ask, "If someone gives you a gift, is it right to despise it?" The point is that too lax a view of the Sabbath fails to see that God has made the Sabbath for our good. If we neglect it, we will miss the good he intends it to bring us.

**Question 6.** Be sure the group sees how the Pharisees' rigidity in keeping the law actually leads them to abuse it far worse than even they think Jesus does. Their rigidity leads to hate and murder.

**Question 7.** Non-Christians are not the only ones who object to our beliefs and practices. Sometimes our most vigorous opposition comes from those who are religious, who resemble the Pharisees of Jesus' day. Be sure to consider objections both groups might have. Jesus tried to help the Pharisees look at the intent of the law. They interpreted the law so rigidly that people got trampled underfoot. Jesus looked behind laws to see how they were intended for our benefit. Jesus was people-centered. The Pharisees were law-centered. This distinction can guide our behavior as Christians as well as our responses to those who object to our behavior.

**Question 11.** Everyone seems to know about someone who wanders about convinced that they have blasphemed the Holy Spirit and are forever condemned. Two points are worth making: (1) Jesus seems always ready to forgive any sin we are ready to confess; (2) the people here who are warned about blaspheming the Holy Spirit are about the last people who are concerned that this might be their problem. Blaspheming the Holy Spirit thus seems to be hardening one's heart against Jesus to the point that one never seeks forgiveness.

**Question 14.** Earlier in this passage we saw that the Pharisees had a rigid attitude toward God's commandments and other people. They evidently viewed themselves merely as God's slaves or subjects. This question helps us to explore how viewing ourselves as part of God's family can keep us from the error of the Pharisees.

### Study 5. Kingdom Parables. Mark 4:1-34.

*Purpose:* To gain insight into the nature of God's kingdom and how we can become better, more creative evangelists.

**Question 2.** Be sure the group notices how many times the words *listen, hear* or *hearing* occur.

**Question 3.** Jesus doesn't consistently describe hearers as either soil or plants. Don't get bogged down in this. Just look at what happens to each combination.

**Question 4.** The parables clearly had the potential to conceal truth as well as to reveal it, and Jesus likely used parables to accomplish both ends. But it is not consistent with Jesus' character that his ultimate goal was to conceal the truth. The Isaiah passage Jesus quotes (Is 6:9-10) highlights Isaiah's responsibility to keep on proclaiming the truth despite the people's refusal to hear it. In a broader context we can see at least two ways that parables served Jesus' purposes. First, they weeded out people who were really not interested, as the group should see in questions 5-6. Second, they had the potential to break through resistance to the truth, as Nathan's parable succeeded in breaking through David's defenses about his adultery with Bathsheba (2 Sam 12:1-14). Had Nathan confronted David directly, he might well have lost his head. By telling the parable Nathan succeeded in getting David to condemn his own actions. Encourage the group to keep watching how Jesus uses parables throughout the Gospel.

**Questions 5-6.** In light of the problem raised in question 4, these questions are designed to explore how people get to be on the inside or the outside (see also 3:34). Regardless of how we understand the role of God's sovereignty in this process, it is clear that individuals have a responsibility to act on what they are hearing.

**Question 7.** In saying "to you has been given the secret of the kingdom," Jesus may mean no more than that he is about to explain the parable to those around him. Three factors, however, suggest that the secret of the kingdom is embedded within the parable of the sower: (1) Jesus' indication that this parable somehow unlocks all the rest (v. 13), (2) the fact that Jesus' remarks about the secret are sandwiched between the parable and its explanation, and (3) the amount of attention given to the parable and its explanation. Two strong possibilities arise from this understanding. First, the secret of the kingdom may be that Jesus is the farmer, the one who brings the kingdom by sowing the word. Second, the secret of the kingdom may be hearing the word and responding to it appropriately, that is, hearing the word, accepting it and acting on it, just as those who are asking for an explanation are doing. If the group is unable to reach a consensus, encourage them to keep thinking this over throughout their study of Mark.

**Question 10.** Be sure the group wrestles with the fact that the farmer does not know on what kind of soil he has scattered the seed until after he has scattered it. So he scatters the seed lavishly everywhere. Often in our evangelism we will discover that the seed we sow grows in some surprising soil. We are not called to judge the soil before we sow. What we once thought to be a hardened path may show itself in a new situation to be good soil.

### Study 6. Desperate Straits. Mark 4:35—6:6.

*Purpose:* To explore how different kinds of fear and faith interact, and to learn how we can better turn our fears into faith.

This passage is long, but if you keep the group moving and focusing on the big picture, you can cover it in the time allotted.

**Questions 3-4.** Some group members may be disturbed by what happened to the pigs and will bring it up early on in the study. If so, don't hesitate to go to question 5 first and then come back to these.

**Question 6.** The purpose of this question is to get people thinking about why Jesus sometimes works to conceal his identity and at other times encourages that it be broadcast. A definite answer requires looking at the whole Gospel, so people should only explore a tentative solution at this point. Geography and who he's speaking to are probably relevant factors. Here Jesus is speaking to a Gentile in a gentile area. In previous instances he has silenced either demons or people in Jewish areas. (This question ties into the issue that scholars refer to as the Messianic secret in Mark.)

**Question 8.** A little thought should convince the group that the questions people are asking and the offense they are taking are an outgrowth of fear.

**Question 9.** This question is designed to get group members to see that fear, like other human emotions, is not something we can turn on and off like a water spigot. What matters is what we *do* in the face of fear. Do we back away from God in our fear, or do we turn toward him? So the same fear may be good or bad depending on how we respond to it.

**Question 12.** Be sure the group notices the threat of death in each incident here.

**Question 13.** This question is designed to help the group to keep tying the Gospel together. Their study will be richer, and they will be much better prepared for the summary study if they keep trying to see the Gospel as a whole as they go along rather than as a series of isolated units.

### Study 7. Understanding the Loaves. Mark 6:6-52.

*Purpose:* To see how a proper vision of Jesus can keep our hearts soft and counteract the effects of burnout.

**Question 2.** If necessary, break this question down. If the disciples take no provisions for themselves, on whom must they rely? What were they to preach? What were they to do if they met resistance? Shaking the dust off their feet in leaving would have been a strong symbolic gesture of rejection— "Keep your own dust!"

**Question 4.** Herod shows symptoms of seed sown both among thorns and in rocky soil. What does this breakdown of categories suggest about the kinds of responses we may get as we share the good news of the kingdom?

**Question 5.** This is a tough question, but a significant one. The word *repent* or *repentance* occurs only three times in Mark's Gospel, yet each time it defines or summarizes a key aspect of the ministry of the person described. In 1:4 we see John the forerunner "preaching a baptism of repentance." In 1:15 we learn that Jesus' ministry was characterized by calling people to repent. Now we learn that those Jesus called to follow him went out and "preached that people should repent." Perhaps readers are wondering what happens to people who go out calling others to repent. *What happened to John?* (Here's the answer.) *What eventually happened to Jesus?* (Believers will already know.) *What then can his followers expect?*

**Question 8.** Herod, like the Pharisees, fails to be the kind of shepherd God desires for his people. Much of Mark's description of Jesus' feeding of the 5,000 uses language similar to that of Ezekiel 34:1-16. Thus we see Jesus fulfilling God's promise to come and be a shepherd to his people. We see this more clearly as readers of the Gospel than Jesus' contemporaries did, but this was one of the ways Jesus was revealing his true identity.

**Question 10.** The group may have trouble answering this question. If so, ask, "What should the feeding of the 5,000 from five loaves have revealed about Jesus?" Had the disciples understood Jesus' true identity, how might their reaction to his walking on the water have been different? This passage is full of allusions from the Old Testament like that of Ezekiel 34 mentioned in question 8. Jesus again and again does what only God did there—stilling the storm (Ps 107:23-32), feeding the crowd in the wilderness (Ex 16) and walking on water (Job 9:8-11). Those with eyes to see should be starting to understand who Jesus really is.

**Study 8. Violating Tradition. Mark 6:53—7:37.**

*Purpose:* To see how tradition can harden our hearts to God's truth and how Jesus' assessment of human need cuts across the distinction between Jew and Gentile.

**Question 2.** Jesus goes about healing and making others clean by his contact with them. The Pharisees see themselves as becoming unclean through their contact with others. What happens in our contact with the world? Are we changing it, or is it changing us?

**Question 7.** If after some time for thought, the group is still struggling with this question, ask, "What aspect of our relationship with God do the ceremonial law and traditions emphasize—the external or the internal? What aspect does Jesus' standard emphasize? Jews and Gentiles obviously differ on the external issues, but do they differ on the internal issues?"

**Questions 8-9.** If the group has trouble with question 8, make sure they identify who the children are, who the dogs are and what the bread is. Then the parable should be clear.

Many people are offended by Jesus' reference to Gentiles as dogs, a term probably as offensive as calling Blacks "niggers." But it is important to see that Jesus uses the sentiment of his countrymen to overturn their racism. Don't allow the group to miss the fact that this woman is the only person who ever replies to one of Jesus' parables with a parable.

**Study 9. Who Do You Say I Am? Mark 8:1—9:1.**

*Purpose:* To have each member of the group confront personally the issue of who Jesus is and what difference he should make in our lives.

**Question 4.** What evidence have the Pharisees shown that they would recognize a sign if one were given?

**Question 5.** If the group has trouble answering this, ask what Jesus condemned the Pharisees for in Mark 7 and what Herod's basic problem was in Mark 6.

**Question 7.** The purpose of this question is just to get the group to notice that the healing occurred in two stages. The significance of this observation is explored in question 12.

**Question 8.** The group may wonder why people would say that Jesus was

Elijah. As we saw in study one, Malachi had prophesied that Elijah would come before the day of the Lord (Mal 4:5). As a result, the Jews of Jesus' day expected a prophet like Elijah to come before the Messiah.

**Question 10.** Peter's view of the Christ (or the Messiah) was likely that of his fellow Jews who expected a political leader, someone who would liberate them from Roman rule and restore their national pride. Such a view left no room for suffering and death.

**Question 12.** We are so used to seeing Peter's confession as a clear realization of who Jesus is that we often fail to see that only gradually did he learn what all it meant. Peter's understanding needed a second touch as well.

**Looking ahead.** For purposes of group discussion it is essential that each group member prepare individually for the next review study.

### Study 10. Review. Mark 1—8.

*Purpose:* To summarize and explore the implications of what the group has discovered about the gospel and the kingdom thus far.

**Question 1.** Be sure the group catches the kingdom focus of the gospel as Jesus proclaimed it.

**Question 4.** If the group seems stumped, you might press further as follows: "Howard Snyder, in *Liberating the Church* (IVP), observes that 'too often the way the church practices evangelism is like a nation in wartime drafting its young men into the army—and then sending them all back home to do as they please' (p. 24). How would seeing Jesus as king and calling people to allegiance to him and his kingdom counteract an accept-Jesus-into-your-heart-and-do-as-you-please attitude?"

**Question 7.** If the group has trouble answering, you could explain that most Jews were looking for a political Messiah, someone to lead them in overthrowing the Romans. What might have happened if Jesus had gone about announcing himself as the Messiah or Christ? Then, too, apart from a history of his deeds, what would have happened had he gone about announcing that he was God?

For advanced groups you may wish to delve deeper into Jesus' use of the phrase "Son of Man." Jesus has used the phrase "the Son of Man" four times so far (2:10, 28; 8:31, 38). With hindsight it is rather easy to see that Jesus was speaking about himself and alluding to his role as Messiah. Jesus' hearers, however, would not likely have heard him that way. To them the phrase "Son of Man" would likely have sounded like another way of saying *man* (as in Psalm 8:4, where it means just that). Thus 2:28 might have sounded like this: "The Sabbath was made for man, not man for the Sabbath. So man is lord even of the Sabbath." Only gradually would it have dawned on people that Jesus was talking about himself. Why might Jesus have spoken of himself in this roundabout way? What specifics thus far has Jesus revealed about himself in this way? How might this tie in with the question of why Jesus tries to silence some people he heals and encourages others to tell what he has done?

## Part 2: Why Did Jesus Come?

### Study 1. Suffering and Glory. Mark 9:2-32.

*Purpose:* To examine the relationship between suffering and glory, human weakness and divine power.

**Question 1.** At least five events present themselves as possible fulfillments of Jesus' prediction—the transfiguration, the resurrection, the ascension, the day of Pentecost and the Second Coming. The Second Coming is the only one of these not to occur within the time frame Jesus mentions. All the rest anticipate the full glory of the Second Coming, giving glimpses of the power that will be fully revealed then. Study 12 will ask the group to consider yet another possible fulfillment of this prophecy.

**Question 2.** Moses and Elijah are representative of the Law and the prophets. What company then does this put Jesus in? The prophecies of Deuteronomy 18:14-22 and Malachi 4:5 reveal even further significance in their presence.

**Question 4.** Be sure the group sees that listening involves obedience. When your mother used to ask you, "Did you hear me?" she wasn't asking a question about your hearing ability but about your obedience.

**Question 5.** If the group has difficulty answering this question, remind them of how we saw in study one that John the Baptist was fulfilling the role of Elijah as predicted in Malachi. Then look at what happened to John in Mark 6:14-29. Lane comments, "It is necessary to assume that the phrase 'even as it is written of him' has reference to the prophet Elijah in the framework of his historical ministry (for example, see 1 Kings 19:2, 10). No passage of Scripture associates suffering with Elijah's eschatological ministry" (William L. Lane, *Commentary on the Gospel of Mark* [Grand Rapids, Mich.: Eerdmans, 1974], p. 326).

**Question 12.** Note especially that the young boy appeared to suffer to the point of death before he was restored.

### Study 2. The First and the Last. Mark 9:33-50.

*Purpose:* To explore the ways self-judgment and a servant attitude can promote Christian unity.

**Question 3.** Be sure the group sees Jesus as the supreme example of the servant destined to be the greatest of all.

**Question 9.** The group may have trouble answering this question. If so, you might ask, "Would cutting off a hand or foot really keep us from sinning? If not, what would?" Sometimes we "spiritualize" Jesus' words to make them easier on ourselves, but spiritualizing here doesn't soften Jesus' words. The point is that it would be well worth plucking out an eye or cutting off a foot if that would keep us from sinning. But the effect would only be to produce blind and lame sinners. The root of our problem lies deeper, and we must confront it there.

**Question 10.** Fire in the earlier verses is clearly linked with judgment or testing. Salt is a common image for purification. How then are Christians purified by judgment or testing?

**Question 11.** If the group has trouble answering the first part of the question, move them on to the second part by asking, "Jesus seems to link having salt in yourselves with being at peace with one another. Does that shed any light on what having salt in yourself might mean?" The group should see that judging ourselves rather than one another contributes to peace and unity.

**Study 3. Divorce, Children and Eternal Life. Mark 10:1-31.**
*Purpose:* To explore some of the moral and social implications of the gospel

**Question 3.** The group may have some strong feelings about this issue. Try to help them to listen to one another and to support their conclusions from the passage. A possible alternative to the view that Jesus intended an absolute prohibition of divorce is that he meant only to assert God's ideal for marriage—an ideal that he recognized that fallen human beings would not always live up to. He thus spoke in exaggerated terms meant to *discourage* all divorce in principle but not to *prohibit* divorce in every circumstance. Although no exceptions are included in Mark's account, Matthew records a slightly different version of Jesus' words, which is not cast in absolute terms (Mt 19:9). The group may want to explore the significance of this difference, but be careful not to spend too much time on this issue.

**Question 4.** "According to rabbinic law a man could commit adultery against another married man by seducing his wife (Deut 22:13-29) and a wife could commit adultery against her husband by infidelity, but a husband could not be said to commit adultery against his wife. . . . This sharp intensifying of the concept of adultery had the effect of elevating the status of the wife to the same dignity as her husband and placed the husband under an obligation of fidelity" (Lane, *Commentary on the Gospel of Mark,* p. 357). Lane also notes that Jewish law did not recognize the right of a woman to divorce her husband, though Roman law did (p. 358).

**Questions 6-7.** The man seeks a response in terms of *activity* meriting eternal life. Ultimately Jesus gives him an answer that is based on *relationship*—"Come, follow me." Yet that relationship is not devoid of social implications.

**Questions 8-9.** Of course, Jesus' illustration points to the fact that it is not only hard but impossible for the rich to be saved on their own. God must work. This passage highlights a paradox of the gospel—that we contribute nothing to our salvation, but we must give all to be Jesus' disciples. The group may struggle with the implications of Jesus' command to the rich man to "go, sell everything you have and give to the poor." Two extremes probably should be avoided: (1) assuming this command is universal and applies to all would-be disciples and (2) assuming that the problem is purely one of attitude and that would-be disciples who love the Lord more than their wealth may keep it. Don't let the group get off easy on this issue.

**Study 4. Blindness and Sight. Mark 10:32-52.**
*Purpose:* To emphasize the servant role in Christian discipleship.
**Question 5.** The Old Testament speaks frequently of the cup of God's wrath (see, for example, Ps 75:8 and Is 51:17-23). Lane notes that "in popular Greek usage the vocabulary of baptism was used to speak of being overwhelmed by disaster or danger" (*Commentary on the Gospel of Mark,* p. 380).
**Question 9.** Don't overlook what Bartimaeus is able to "see" about Jesus even though he is blind.

**Study 5. Palm Sunday. Mark 11:1-25.**
*Purpose:* To better understand righteous anger and how a spirit of forgiveness is necessary when praying for God's judgment.
**Question 3.** Jesus here is clearly fulfilling Zechariah's prophecy about the Messiah's entry into Jerusalem (Zech 9:9-10). Surprisingly, at least to most Jews of Jesus' day, he comes as a man of peace, riding on a donkey rather than a warhorse.
**Question 4.** Be sure the group notices what the people did as well as what they said.

Despite how clearly we can see that Jesus was entering Jerusalem as Messiah, the people looking on probably did not. They undoubtedly saw Jesus as an important person, but may have seen him only as an important teacher on a special mission to Jerusalem. Their shouts, though loaded with messianic significance, were excerpts from Psalm 118 and other songs sung regularly on

# 92

Mark: Follow Me

the way to Jerusalem each spring and fall for the major festivals. For further details, see Lane's *Commentary on the Gospel of Mark,* pp. 393-94, 396-97.
**Question 5.** For the context of Jesus' comments from the Old Testament, see Isaiah 56:4-8 and Jeremiah 7:1-11.
**Question 7.** Fig trees and vines are often used as symbols of Israel's faithfulness to God. God comes to his vineyard looking for grapes and figs, that is, righteousness and justice and mercy. Thus looking for fruit on the fig tree represents what Jesus is looking for in the temple. See, for example, Jeremiah 8:13 (RSV, the NIV obscures this verse); 29:17; Hosea 9:10-16; Joel 1:7; Micah 7:1-6.

The group is apt to struggle with why Jesus curses the fig tree when "it was not the season for figs." It is probably most helpful to see this as an acted parable of the judgment that the temple faces. For those being judged, judgment seldom comes when expected.
**Question 10.** The Zechariah passage is 14:1-11. Note that this understanding of prayer to move mountains is consistent with the judgment theme found in the incidents in the temple and with the fig tree.

### Study 6. Tempting Questions. Mark 11:27—12:27.
*Purpose:* To better understand the role of answering and asking questions in Christian discipleship.
**Question 5.** The scripture Jesus cited was Psalm 118:22-23. It "refers to one of the building blocks gathered at the site of Solomon's Temple which was rejected in the construction of the Sanctuary but which proved to be the keystone to the porch" (Lane, *Commentary on the Gospel of Mark,* p. 420). Modern distinctions between cornerstones, keystones and capstones will likely confuse the issue here. NIV's "capstone" is probably the least satisfactory translation of the Greek since it often connotes a finishing stone without structural significance. Either a keystone or cornerstone—either of which is vitally linked to the structural soundness of the building or arch—is meant.
**Question 7.** The Roman denarius brought to Jesus likely bore the inscription "Tiberius Caesar Augustus, Son of the Divine Augustus." Lane comments, "By recognizing the relative autonomy of the civil authority in the first part of his response Jesus showed himself opposed to any belief in an essentially theocratic state and to any expectation of an imminent eschatological consummation of his own mission. But by distinguishing so sharply between Caesar and God he tacitly protested against the idolatrous claims advanced on the coins" (*Commentary on the Gospel of Mark,* p. 424).
**Question 12.** Jesus' answer to the Sadducees in verse 26 is not as weak as

might first sound to modern ears. The formula "the God of Abraham, the God of Isaac, and the God of Jacob" is a reminder of God's covenant faithfulness. Lane summarizes, "It is inconceivable that God would provide for the patriarchs some partial tokens of deliverance and leave the final word to death, of which all the misfortunes and sufferings of human existence are only a foretaste. If the death of the patriarchs is the last word of their history, there has been a breach of the promises of God guaranteed by the covenant, and of which the formula 'the God of Abraham, of Isaac, and of Jacob' is the symbol" (*Commentary on the Gospel of Mark,* p. 430).

**Study 7. An End to Questions. Mark 12:28-44.**
*Purpose:* To underscore the relationship between love for God and love for neighbor and to further explore who Jesus is.
**Question 3.** The teacher is drawing together insights from 1 Samuel 15:22; Proverbs 21:3 and Hosea 6:6.
**Question 7.** Jesus is quoting David's words from Psalm 110:1. Be sure the group understands clearly that only a Christ who is both fully human and fully divine can be both lord and descendant.
**Question 13.** We saw in study one that Mark saw the coming of John the Baptist and Jesus in light of Malachi 3:1. This question shows us again Mark's concern to see Jesus as a fulfiller of prophecy.

**Study 8. Keep Watch. Mark 13:1-37.**
*Purpose:* To better understand Jesus' predictions concerning the fall of Jerusalem and his return, and to explore what it means to be alert for his return.
**Questions 2-3.** Make sure the group notices that the disciples are asking about the destruction of the temple. Jesus' answer is broader than their question; he enlarges the discussion to include the end (the last things).
**Question 6.** Because the issue here is complicated and many people have definite views, this question is designed to help the group appreciate the strength of different points of view. It isn't necessary to achieve consensus on this issue; questions 9-12 get at the crucial issue.
    Even expert opinion is divided on these issues. Lane notes that Luke, without mentioning "the abomination that causes desolation," clearly points to the events of A.D. 70 with armies surrounding Jerusalem. Josephus attributes the destruction of the temple to abuses of the Zealots who held up there from fall to spring A.D. 67-68. He accuses them of all sorts of crimes and wandering about in the Holy of Holies, even committing murder there. He sees the culmination of these abuses ("the abomination that causes desola-

tion") in vesting as high priest a low-class priest by the name of Phanni. I
is possible that many early Christians would have sympathized with Jose
phus's sentiment. (See Lane's *Commentary on the Gospel of Mark,* p. 469, a
well as the whole discussion on pp. 465-73.)

F. F. Bruce holds that Josephus caricatures the Zealots and that his testi
mony is not to be trusted. He sees fulfillment of the "abomination that cause
desolation" in the Roman sacrifices offered at the temple court at its destruc
tion. (See F. F. Bruce, *New Testament History* [Garden City, N.Y.: Doubleday
1969], pp. 257-383.)

Lane and Bruce differ on the details while agreeing that "the abominatior
that causes desolation" has already appeared in the temple during the event
culminating in the destruction of the temple in A.D. 70. A further fulfillment
still to come, may parallel the events described in 2 Thessalonians 2:3-4 wher
the "man of lawlessness . . . sets himself up in God's temple, proclaiming
himself to be God" or when he performs some act of desecration (see Rober
L. Thomas, "1, 2 Thessalonians," in *The Expositor's Bible Commentary,* ed
Frank E. Gaebelein [Grand Rapids, Mich.: Zondervan, 1978], 11:322).

**Question 8.** This question is designed to bring out the *cosmic* character o
the distress in verses 24-27 in contrast to the *local* character of those in verse
5-23. This is one piece of evidence that may suggest a difference in time
between the destruction of Jerusalem and the return of Christ. One way tc
view the structure of Mark 13 is as follows:

1. 13:1-23—description of local signs associated with "these things," the
destruction of the temple.

2. 13:24-27—description of cosmic signs associated with "that day," the
return of Christ.

3. 13:28-31—the surety that the temple will be destroyed within a gener
ation.

4. 13:32-36—the uncertainty of when Christ will return.

**Questions 10-12.** Regardless of how we resolve the question of signs anc
of timing, Jesus above all urges us to be ready. Here is a point on which the
group should clearly agree.

### Study 9. The Betrayer Approaches. Mark 14:1-42.

*Purpose:* To empathize with Jesus in his last hours before the crucifixion and
to explore a variety of discipleship issues: priorities, the Lord's Supper, the
necessity of Jesus' death, and human failure.

**Question 2.** This question may be answered in part by responses to question
1, but be sure to explore the legitimacy of some of the objections, especially

light of Jesus' own teaching.

**Question 3.** The issue, of course, is whether it is ever right to spend money n stained glass, pipe organs, padded pews and carpeting for our places of orship while some people in the world are going hungry. It is unlikely that e group will reach consensus in a short time. The question is intended to ise the issue and provoke thought. Don't spend too much time on this.

**Question 8.** Notice that Jesus here again is an example of what he is asking f his disciples.

The spirit in verse 38 may be the Holy Spirit. If so, Jesus' words here are reminder to the disciples of the resources that are theirs as they confront eir own weakness.

## tudy 10. Betrayed! Mark 14:43-72.

*urpose:* To explore the variety of motives involved in Jesus' betrayal and pandonment, and to draw warnings and encouragement for times of our own ssting as disciples.

**Question 4.** In trying to save himself, the young man loses what little he has. pme have thought this young man was Mark himself, included anonymously n this account of Jesus' betrayal.

**Question 6.** In identifying himself as the Christ, Jesus goes on to link himself ith "the Son of Man" described in Daniel 7:13-14. This is the first time his ublic use of the title "Son of Man" would have had clear messianic over-ones.

Sometime on their own, advanced groups may wish to review Jesus' use f the term "Son of Man" throughout the whole Gospel. For the use of this rm in Mark 1—8, see the note on question 7 in study ten. What further sights into the questions asked there are seen through the use of "Son of an" in the last half of Mark (9:9, 12, 31; 10:33; 13:26; 14:21, 41)?

**Question 8.** The issue here is that if Jesus was not God, he was clearly guilty f blasphemy.

## tudy 11. Victory Snatched from Defeat. Mark 15:1—16:8.

*urpose:* To better understand the significance of Christ's death in order to rengthen our commitment to sharing the gospel with others.

**Questions 2-4.** Questions 2-3 may be answered by the group in responding o question 1. If so, you might want to reword question 4 as follows: "How in we keep from succumbing to Pilate's temptation of wanting to do right ut not doing it?"

**Question 6.** If the group has difficulty seeing the relevance of 10:38 and

14:36, ask, "If Jesus had been drugged, how would it have blunted his full participation in the cup of suffering he voluntarily took on?"

**Question 7.** Note especially "he saved others, . . . but he can't save himself." Be sure the group sees that it is precisely *because* he did not save himself that he is able to save others. There are several other ironies in the passage. Take time to answer this key question fully.

**Question 8.** Skip this question if the group has not prepared ahead of time.

**Question 9.** While the centurion's confession may not have been a full-blown testimony of faith, he is not saying Jesus was merely "a son of God" as some translations suggest. No article is present in the Greek because the predicate noun comes first just as in John 1:1 (the Word was God). (See Lane' *Commentary on the Gospel of Mark*, p. 571, n. 69.)

**Question 13.** Two issues come to the fore here. First, why does the Gospel seem to come to such an inconclusive close? The group may be helped in thinking about why this might be appropriate by reconsidering how Mark opens his Gospel (1:1). The second issue concerns ending the Gospel on a note of fear. But as we have seen, especially in study 6, not all fear is bad. In fact, this last sentence of the Gospel could just as well, if not better, be translated, "They said nothing to anyone, because they were filled with awe." There are several instances in Mark's Gospel of people who respond with fear or awe to significant new revelations (see 4:41; 5:15, 33, 36; 6:50; 9:6, 32). Thus the Gospel ends on a note of awe and wonder at what God has done.

**Looking ahead.** Be sure to encourage your group to prepare in advance for next week's review.

### Study 12. Review. Mark 9—16.

*Purpose:* To summarize and explore the implications of the last half of Mark's Gospel.

Don't skip this review! At least not if you want to get the most out of your time in Mark. The rewards of looking back and drawing together certain themes are well worth the effort.

**Question 5.** If the group fails to consider the cross as a key display of Jesus' glory, you may want to ask at what points Jesus' identity as the Son of God is declared and recognized (see 1:1, 11; 9:7; 14:61-62 and 15:39).

**Question 6.** In answering this question, as in answering question 5, it is key to see that the centurion sees Jesus' glory (his identity) on the cross (15:39).

*James Hoover, a former campus staff member with Inter-Varsity Christian Fellowship, is an associate editor with InterVarsity Press.*